DO YOU KNOW?

Level 2

EARTH

Written by Nick Coates
Series Editor: Nick Coates
Designed by Dynamo Limited

LADYBIRD BOOKS

UK | USA | Canada | Ireland | Australia
India | New Zealand | South Africa

Ladybird Books Ltd is part of the Penguin Random House group of companies
whose addresses can be found at global.penguinrandomhouse.com.
www.penguin.co.uk   www.puffin.co.uk   www.ladybird.co.uk

Penguin
Random House
UK

First published 2023
001

Printed in China

The authorized representative in the EEA is Penguin Random House Ireland,
Morrison Chambers, 32 Nassau Street, Dublin D02 YH68

A CIP catalogue record for this book is available from the British Library

ISBN: 978-0-241-62253-7

All correspondence to:
Ladybird Books
Penguin Random House Children's
One Embassy Gardens, 8 Viaduct Gardens, London SW11 7BW

Contents

New words

air
(noun)

around

cut down

erode

grow

land

layer

move

push

rise

rock

sky

Do the continents move?

Earth is our home. The **land** on Earth makes the seven continents.

People live on six of the continents and a very small number of people live on Antarctica. It is very cold there.

Did you know the continents **move**? In the past, they were in different places!

North America

South America

Europe

Asia

North America

Africa

South America

Antarctica

Australia

Europe

Asia

Africa

Australia

Antarctica

🔍 LOOK!

Look at the pages. Which continent do you live on?
Which is the biggest continent? Which is the smallest?

Where did Pangea go?

Sometimes the continents move away from each other.

Sometimes they move close to each other.

A long time ago, the land was one big continent. Its name was Pangea. But then things changed. The land moved and moved, and the sea came in.

Pangea

This made the seven continents. The continents are still moving today – but not very fast!

Dinosaurs lived on Pangea.

📋 PROJECT

Work with a friend. Find out about different types of dinosaurs that lived on Pangea.

Do mountains grow?

Mountains are very tall. Some **grow** every year.

This is because the land is moving.

mountain

When continents **push** each other, some of the land goes up.

The Himalayan mountains grow 10 millimetres every year.

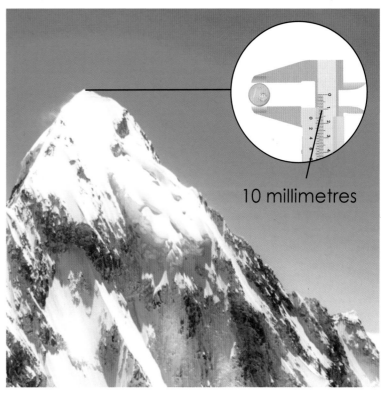

10 millimetres

▶ WATCH!

Watch the video (see page 32).
On what continent are the Himalayan mountains?

What are rainbow mountains?

Rainbow mountains are mountains with many colours. The colours are different **layers** of **rock**. These mountains are pink, yellow and green.

These people are on the Rainbow Mountains in Peru.

You can see the layers in these rocks.

Zhangye Mountains, China

📖 FIND OUT!

Use books or the internet to find out what gives the different layers of rock their colours.

What makes a canyon?

Mountains go up. Canyons go down. There is usually a river in a canyon.

The river makes the canyon. Rivers are always moving. The water **erodes** the rocks.

The Grand Canyon, USA

The Grand Canyon is very big. You can walk in it, travel on a boat or fly there.

The Antelope Canyon is very beautiful.

Antelope Canyon, USA

Charyn Canyon, Kazakhstan

▶ WATCH!

Watch the video (see page 32).

What is at the bottom of the Grand Canyon?

15

What is inside a cave?

Caves can be inside mountains.
Water often erodes rock to make caves.

Caves can be very big and beautiful.
Stalagmites and stalactites
grow inside the caves.

Caves are important homes
for many plants and animals.

Cayman Crystal Caves,
Cayman Islands

Stalagmites grow up.
Stalactites grow down.

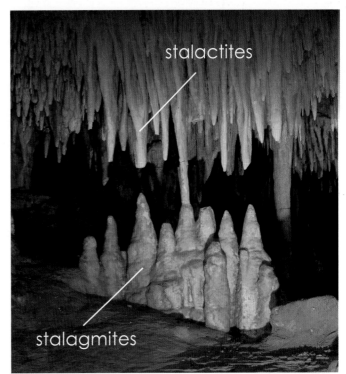

stalactites

stalagmites

Bats like to
sleep in caves.

📖 FIND OUT!

Use books or the internet. What is it called
when a stalagmite and a stalactite meet?

What lives in the soil?

There is a layer of soil on the Earth. It is where plants grow. We can grow flowers in the soil in gardens. A lot of things live in the soil.

earthworm

soil

There are very many earthworms in the soil. They help to make good soil.

Big animals live in the soil, too.

grub

fungi

bacteria

📋 PROJECT

Work with a friend. Choose a small area of soil.
Use books or the internet to find ways of bringing
earthworms to the surface. Count the earthworms!

19

Why do we need forests?

A forest is land with many trees. There are different kinds of forests in different parts of the world. But they all help to clean our **air** and water.

Rainforests grow where it is hot and wet.

Many different kinds of animals and plants live in rainforests. It is their home, too.

💭 THINK!

Is there a forest near to you?
What can you do there?

Deforestation is a big problem today.
People **cut down** forests and make farms,
roads or towns on the land. There is no
place for the plants and animals to live.
The trees cannot clean our air.
This is bad for us and for the Earth.

Some people plant trees
to make new forests.

📖 FIND OUT!

Use the internet or ask people you know.
Where are people planting trees near you?

What is an island?

An island is land with water all **around** it. Some are very small with one or two trees and birds. But some are very big with towns and cities for many people.

Sometimes people make islands, for example this island in Dubai.

Tuvalu

The sea is **rising**. Some islands are going under the sea.

Loreto Island, Italy

▶ WATCH!

Watch the video (see page 32).
Why is the sea rising? What can happen to islands?

Where can we find coral reefs?

Corals are very small animals. They live in the sea. They live together in coral reefs. Some coral reefs are very big.

Great Barrier Reef, Queensland, Australia

coral reef

Lots of fish live around coral reefs.

This sea turtle also lives near a coral reef.

coral

🔍 LOOK!

Look at the pages. What animals live near coral reefs?

What colours can we see in the sky?

In some places, we can sometimes see beautiful colours in the **sky**. These are auroras.

Sometimes, a wind from the Sun moves the air on Earth. This makes different colours. They move and change.

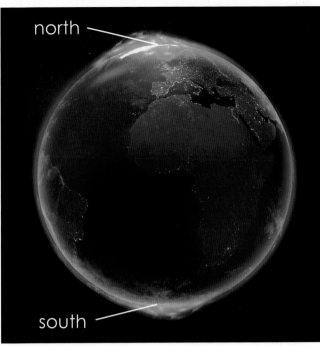

north

south

We see auroras at the north and south of Earth.

We can also see them from above Earth.

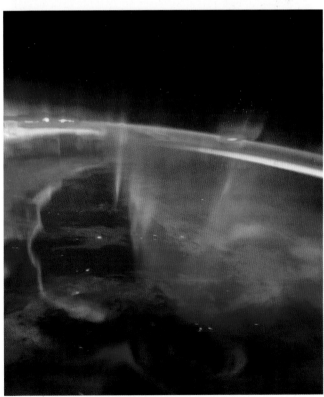

🔍 LOOK!

Look at the pages. What colours can you see in the sky?

Quiz

Choose the correct answers.

1 The Himalayan mountains grow . . . in a year.
   a 1 millimetre
   b 10 millimetres
   c 100 millimetres

2 What do you usually find in a canyon?
   a a river
   b a mountain
   c a cave

3 We find caves . . .
   a in rivers.
   b in the soil.
   c inside mountains.

4 Earthworms live in . . .
   a soil.
   b caves.
   c deserts.

5 Deforestation is when . . .
   a people plant a lot of trees.
   b people grow a lot of trees.
   c people cut down a lot of trees.

6 Around an island, you can see . . .
   a forests.
   b water.
   c mountains.

7 Coral reefs are . . .
   a in mountains.
   b in the sky.
   c under the sea.

8 We see auroras at the . . . of Earth.
   a north and south
   b east and west
   c left and right

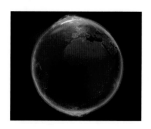

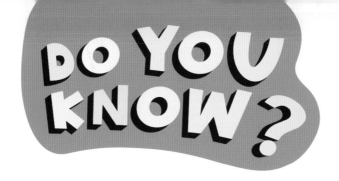

DO YOU KNOW?

Visit www.ladybirdeducation.co.uk for
FREE **DO YOU KNOW?** teaching resources.

- video clips with simplified voiceover and subtitles
- video and comprehension activities
- class projects and lesson plans
- audio recording of every book
- digital version of every book
- full answer keys

To access video clips, audio tracks and digital books:

1 Go to **www.ladybirdeducation.co.uk**
2 Click 'Unlock book'
3 Enter the code below

aZc3y091t0

Stay safe online! Some of the DO YOU KNOW? activities ask children to do extra research online. Remember:

- ensure an adult is supervising;
- use established search engines such as Google or Kiddle;
- children should never share personal details, such as name, home or school address, telephone number or photos.